Transplant

Transplant

*"The Right Connection
Makes All The Difference"*

Richard Zamora

XULON PRESS

Xulon Press
555 Winderley Pl, Suite 225
Maitland, FL 32751
407.339.4217
www.xulonpress.com

Paperback ISBN-13: 978-1-66289-102-1
Ebook ISBN-13: 978-1-66289-103-8

Table of Contents

Acknowledgements

I would like to express my special thanks to author/writer John Maxwell for his time and efforts he provided me through the leadership books, his useful advice and suggestions were very helpful to me in completing this book, I am eternally grateful for you.

Writing this book was harder than I thought and more rewarding than I could have ever imagined. None of this would have bee*n possible without my wife and best friend Carmen Zamora who has stood by my side and has encouraged me to go beyond all my struggles and health issues.

To all the individuals I have had the opportunity to lead, be led by, or watch their leadership from afar such as Dr. Howard John Wesley for his teachings, Dr. Bonham that performed my liver transplant and all the brothers from Men of Iron and most of all Ricky and Melinda Plaza for sponsoring me to make this book possible.

Thank you to all of you that have been in this faith walk along the way, and for being the inspiration and foundation for this to be possible, God Bless you all, Richard Zamora.

Transplant:

The Right Connection Makes All the Difference

The Power of the Right Connections

Have you ever prayed for someone or something and it didn't happen; have you ever been sick and diagnosed with two years to live? Well, in 2001 my doctors gave me two years to live, and I am writing this book for those who have struggled with themselves and even with God, those who have prayed but had nothing happen. It's also about recovering when something happens to you or your family that came out of nowhere. This book is for those who have had their faith knocked out of balance; I want to say at the beginning that the right connection makes all the difference.

I will share more detail on my experience of not only being sick but also the time when my heart stopped three times, and the things I saw and heard. Now, I strongly believe that whoever is in our inner circle will determine not only how far we will go in life, but also associating ourselves with the wrong groups can keep us not only where we are but can take us moving in circles, without allowing us to move forward.

Before we get into the importance of the power of the right connections in our lives, I want to thank first my wife,

Carmen Zamora. She has been by my side through thick and thin. We have been married forty-one years and together for forty-four years, and besides God, she's the best thing that has come into my life. I would also like to thank Ricky and Melinda Plaza for sponsoring me to be able to write this book. I have been wanting to write this book for years; even during the pandemic in 2020, I was off work for nine months and attempted to write this book but didn't get too far by myself, so without any success it was placed on the back burner.

On February 26, 2021, our men's group, called Men of Iron—which is a men's discipleship group that has been meeting every Monday for six-plus years—had a men's breakfast, and it was at this breakfast that Ricky told me, "Can we chat after the breakfast ends?" As we sat down to talk, he said he felt God had impressed on his heart to ask me, "how do you feel about writing a book? I will sponsor you." I was blown away. I never told him that I've had a desire to write a book. The only one who had known for about ten years is my wife. That's how this book was born, so when I say the right connection makes all the difference, that is based on the book you're about to read. It was influenced and birthed out of having the right connection; most of all, if there's ever an example of having the right connection in our lives, if there was ever the greatest leader to follow, it would be Jesus. Now let me explain, if you read the gospels in the Bible, you will see Jesus had people around Him. For His mission was to choose people who were willing to give up what they had in mind to follow Him, and it was twelve men. Now, on a side note, the funny thing is that Jesus didn't use volunteers, He used people He chose. Too many times in leadership we tend to use people that we feel are qualified, but He hasn't chosen. You see, God doesn't use the qualified, He uses the called—those who know deep down inside they are called for a reason.

Jesus chose twelve men. He chose Peter and Andrew, who were brothers; Jesus said to them, "Follow me and I will make you fish for men" (Matt. 4:18–19). Then verses 21–22 say Jesus saw two brothers, James and John, and as they were sitting in the boat with their father mending their nets: "Jesus called them at once." They didn't think about it. They did not say, "Not now," but the Bible says at once they left not only their boat but their father. As they continued, Jesus chose eight more men who, together with the four previously chosen, became the twelve disciples. We see how Jesus set the example that just being connected to our Heavenly Father is not enough. I believe Jesus set the standard on team building, and we can really learn from Jesus how we need to come along other like-minded people to accomplish the calling, the mission that God has laid before us. Why? Because this kingdom building is bigger than us, it's beyond us, so the question is, how did Jesus choose his team well? We can see it in the Bible, in Luke 6:12–16, it says that Jesus went up to a mountain to pray, and he actually prayed all night; then, at daybreak, he went and chose the disciples, so we see that Jesus realized that in order for the Gospel to continue on after he left he had to make sure he equipped the disciples to do just that; thus, we need to understand just having God in our life is not enough; we need to realize we need to be connected to other Godly people now. Before you get it twisted, let me explain.

In Genesis 2:18 (AMPC) God said, "It is not good (sufficient, satisfactory) that the man should not be alone; I will make him a helper (suitable, adapted, complementary) for him." As we keep reading Genesis 2, in the next part God created animals, and Adam named them, but when it was done, God saw that "there was still not a helper suitable for him." God told Adam to take a nap. God put Adam in a deep sleep and took out one of his rib bones and created woman. Again, we see clearly how the right connection makes all the difference. When God said, "It's not good for man to be alone," he wasn't alone if you think about it, because Adam had God. You see, it's crucial that we are connected to the right people and not to think, "God is all I need"; not true, God was not enough. Yes, He will encourage us, develop us, meet our needs, lead and guide us, and protect us by having the right people around. You see, when we isolate ourselves is when we have a problem regarding certain decisions. Let me explain, when we isolate ourselves and refuse to have that Godly circle of life, we will hear only one voice, and that's our voice; believe me, our own voice, our thoughts, can lead us down the wrong path in life. Why? Because we're always right. We desperately need to have people around us with the right counsel. The right connection can be a matter of life and death; what I'm trying to say when talking about life and death is that it's very important to not just have the right connection in life but to listen to the people God has brought into our life. Why is it so important to listen? Because those that don't hear right don't speak right, and this, my friend, can be a huge honking deal when it comes to our destiny, our future here in this life.

I had a liver transplant, after which my heart stopped three times. I saw and experienced what that ending of life and the beginning journey looks like, and even feels like, which you will read about more in this book. After years of being sick and on my deathbed, I received my liver transplant. Right after having this transplant, the doctor, Doctor Bonham at Stanford

Hospital in Palo Alto, California, told me in the recovery room that in all the years of doing transplants, he had never seen a liver connection take such as mine.dr Bonham said I quote, "The minute we connected the liver, with my very own eyes I saw a pink wave that went across the liver and it changed color." My body immediately accepted it, it was the right connection.

As we continue on the path we're on, we experience trauma in life because we live in a broken world. When our lives are broken, when our lives are shattered from drug abuse, alcohol addiction, divorce, loss of a loved one too early, the list goes on, you see, we're on the transplant table of life, and the fact is that not everyone heals as fast, and recovery time varies. The question is, what do you do when we're on the transplant table and things we ask for don't happen when weask for it, when we've prayed, and the pain doesn't go away? When evil and tragedy knock on our door, or we pray and ask God to remove the thorn in our flesh, the thorn that keeps popping up, poking us, and reminding us that were not in control as we thought we were?

You see, I believe we can't do it on our own. I believe what makes these heartaches difficult for people is when their wants don't line up with God's will in their lives. When our lives are out of control is when we reach for tangible, seeable things, which is where we create idols. What is an idol? It's someone or something we use to replace God in our life. This is where we have created our own god. Why? Because a god we create is a god we control. When things in life don't seem to happen the way we thought, the way we planned, let's be sure to understand the power of the right connections, and this is where this book comes in. If this book can bring hope to someone who has experienced pain and heartache whether in their marriage, with their kids, or just life itself, then mission accomplished.

CHAPTER ONE

The Connection Is Wrong

(Connected to All the Wrong Things)

A s a kid growing up, things seemed okay. I have a younger brother, and I still remember when we would be out playing, riding bikes, hanging out with our friends, we knew as soon as the streetlights came on it was time to get home. My parents both worked jobs and worked hard at providing things that were needed. Every dinner we all sat together at the dinner table, and as far as I could see my parents, my life was pretty good—until dysfunction knocked at our family's door. My parents separated and then divorced. I was thirteen years old, and this, my friend, rocked my little world. I can remember at times I wanted to stay with my mom, and then I wanted to stay with my dad. My emotions were all over the place. After this, I began to connect to all the wrong things. It started out in high school as a freshman, smoking weed—Thai stick—and then acid. From there I began selling PCP that was being supplied through a family member. Yeah. Crazy, right? I was not going to school to go to class anymore, I was going to school to sell drugs. As the years went on, I began to abuse the drugs I was selling. Years had gone by, and now the very thing I thought I had control of had control of me. Now I'm seventeen years old, working at a car wash, and still connected to all the wrong things.

The next wrong connection I made took me for quite a ride—a ride that now I couldn't stop and was unable to get off on my own—heroin. A cousin of mine told me, "You got to try this!" He fixed me up, and from that point on that's all I lived for. But here's the thing, what we are connected to in life is not only going to affect us, but it will also affect those closest to us: our family, our friends, and so on. When I met my wife in the early '80s, little did she realize what was going to happen. After a few years of living together and two young boys, I was strung out bad; little things started missing from the house such as TVs, washer and dryers, VCRs. You get the picture; I was now robbing from anyone I could. I tried to stop, but I felt "once a dope fiend, always a dope fiend." On a side note, I remember an armed robbery that I was arrested for as a juvenile, and the psych doctor after evaluating me told my mom right in front of me, "There's no hope for your son, he's never going to change." That's stuck to me to this very day, and let me tell you, the words told to us can be deeply connected to our future.

The connection I had with heroin cost me my dignity and my health, and it destroyed my family. In the mid to late 80's I was burning all my bridges fast with people who were trying to help me. I was just flat-out taking advantage of them. My wife started to go to church, and I went here and there, just enough to keep the peace at the house. She was praying for me. People were praying for me, and people were praying for us. I will never forget a young couple that would come over and talk to us. They would always come over and knock on the door to invite us to church, and I thank God for my wife because every time they came over, I would tell my wife, "Tell them I am not here," and as soon as they came in my wife would yell, "Richard, there's someone here to see you." Then I would walk out of the room and say, "Here I come! Hey, how's it going? It's good to see you!" Well, that is a good wife.

I was always making promises to go to church, and I went sometimes less than some, but I went at times; there I was, going to church on a Sunday morning or evening loaded on heroin in church with black Ray-Ban glasses on. You see, I thought I was cool, and no one knew—boy, was I wrong. Well, this went on for a while, and I am ever so grateful for this couple from Victory Outreach San Jose; they never gave up on us. One day my wife told me, "You have to leave." She said, "I can't serve God and go to church with you here making it hard for me." Well, I chose drugs over my family and left. I would come by once a week to see my two sons; then, one day when I called to come by and see the kids, my wife told me I can't come to see the kids until I changed my life. This rocked my world because I'd told myself I would never do to my family what my parents did to me. It dawned on me that it was too late. I really hit rock bottom. From this point on I was now sleeping in cars, garages, or abandoned houses—selling dope to use dope—and then it all came to an end. I was tired. I will never forget this day, January 6, 1989, I had a gram of heroin, some reds and quaaludes. I went into a field, shot up all the dope, and took all the pills and sat in the field. No one was around, only me and God, and I started to lay down and fall asleep. That was it. I was going to sleep, never to wake up, never to see my wife, my kids; this was it, and then, by God's

3

grace, I stood up and said, "I don't want to die." All my life I have been connected to all the wrong things. I stumbled from the field into an open garage door and jumped on a bike that was lying in the garage. I rode for miles across town, and the only place I knew of where I felt I could go—the only hope I had—was the church. I believe the church is still today the hope for the world. I got to the Victory Outreach San Jose Church where finally I was connecting to the right thing—the right source—and that was God.

I remember it so well. It was a Friday night church service, and it was just ending. As I walked into the church, Pastor Ed Morales was in the lobby. He was just coming out of the sanctuary, and he took one look at me and said, "You need to get out of this city." There was a guy there at the church I will never forget; he took me to Sacramento, California, to the Christian rehab home. When Victory Outreach dropped me off, it was 1:30 a.m. , and now the connection was right. Well here I am in the detox center and God helped me I kicked heroin; well, let me explain how this was possible, after two weeks in the detox home I went to church with the other fellas that were in the same boat I was. Sitting there in service, I remember it well, as the preacher who was sharing seemed as if he were talking to me, and then I began to cry, trying my hardest to hold it back as tears flowed down my cheek; then, at the end is where the right connection took place. There was a call to come up for prayer after the end of the service, and I went up, and as soon as I got to the altar I began to weep like a baby and then fell to my knees, weeping uncontrollably; then the preacher came up to me and said, "Stand up." He looked at me and said, "For sure today God has delivered you from drugs and alcohol."

As soon as he said that I felt as if someone had thrown a bucket of honey on me, and as it ran down me, I felt like a vibration throughout my whole body, and it felt so good, it was like for once in my life I felt free. Since then, I have been free from heroin addiction. Have I made mistakes? Yes. Will I make more mistakes? Yes, but one thing I understand is that who the son sets free is free indeed, so no longer did this monster addiction have control over me, but now it was Jesus who took the wheel. Well, one year later I graduated from the Christian rehab home and then began the journey with the connection of connections—the King of Kings and Lord of Lords. Now my involvement in church began. I was involved in church ministry, learning and growing. As I look back on my life, I see how the Lord will put us in charge not for those around us but for God to bring us to certain points in our lives to deal with ourselves. I'm a licensed minister now, trying to get people to choose the right path—the right connection—because at the end of the day the right connection does make all the difference.

Here's the question: Is it possible to build the house of life , adding brick by brick, wall by wall, year by year, get to the top of your life and say, "I am not sure who I have become"? Is it possible to be so close to seeing a future in your mind only to find out this is not the future God had for me? I'm talking now about being connected to people more than being connected to God. Understanding our identity is not in who we are but in what we do now; this is a huge honking problem. Realizing we have to restart our lives, which took years to build, and then to feel it's too late and all because we didn't have the right connection, the right touch? You see, as we go through the transplant table of life, we not only have touched a lot of people, but a lot of people have touched our lives, and prayerfully, we haven't lost touch with the one that touched us in the beginning of this journey, which is the right touch, which is Jesus.

To make a long story longer, "Hello, somebody."

There are the outside influences that affect the decisions that we make; in other words, the people that have touched our lives will be very instrumental for us to move forward, not backward, not back to the things that have had us bound. A good example is the blind man with Jesus in the Bible:

> And they came to Bethsaida. And [people] brought to Him a blind man and begged Him to touch him.
>
> And He caught the blind man by the hand and led him out of the village; and when He had spit on his eyes and put His hands upon him, He asked him, Do you [possibly] see anything?
>
> And he looked up and said, I see people, but [they look] like trees, walking.
>
> Then He put His hands on his eyes again; and the man looked intently [that is, fixed his eyes on definite objects], and he was restored and saw everything distinctly [even what was at a distance].
>
> And He sent him away to his house, telling [him], Do not [even] enter the village *or tell anyone there.* (Mark 8:22–26, AMPC)

I think this passage is a message to the church on being around Jesus but not being able to see Jesus clearly. This man had a lot of people touching him; he was blind, so people guided him, led him, cared for him, and protected him. It is also possible that there may have been some people who took advantage of him, so this man had a lot of hands on him. There's one thing to consider so we avoid being connected to all the wrong people: we need to be connected to the proper people. In the Bible, God puts a lot of emphasis on relationships. God created Adam to have fellowship with; then God said, "It is not good for man to be alone" (Gen. 2:18). But Adam wasn't alone, he had God. Then God said He would make him a helper suitable for him, and God created the animals, and Adam begins to name all the animals. When Adam was done, the Bible says there wasn't a helper suitable for him. Then God put Adam to sleep, and God pulled Eve out of Adam.

On a side note, I believe there are some things that God wants to pull out of us things only he can do. . As we see with Adam, God knew the importance of relationships, the importance of having the right connection. Now, back to the blind man. These men brought the blind man to Jesus. They wanted him to have what they have. Watch out for people who are always taking from you and never depositing. Watch out for people who try to keep you where you're at in life. We need people who will bring us to Jesus, people who will pray for us without asking. One, we need to be connected to the proper people; two, we need to be patient with the process

then we can appreciate not just the destination but the journey. After the people brought the blind man to Jesus, he then took him , let me say it this way, there will be a season of separation: God will remove certain people and certain things that take our focus off Him so we can see more clearly; we're talking about being connected to the wrong people, the wrong things, due to a bad connection. The question is, *How do I know when the connections to the people around me are right?* At the end of Mark 8:26 Jesus connected with him and then told him, "Don't go back into the village on your way home." Jesus gave him wise counsel and good advice, don't go back to the place of your dysfunction.. If it's the right connection we will receive wise counsel, that will direct us not back where we came from but where we're going. Let me leave you with this: if we're connected to the wrong things, we will stay blind and lost depending on people and not God , and the danger of having the wrong hands touching us is that when they leave us, we stay stuck in the same spot.

CHAPTER TWO

Connected to a World of Pain

I t was in the middle of the year 2001, and I found myself going to work, and it seemed as though right after lunch I would feel exhausted. It was as if I had no oxygen in my body. This tired feeling was not normal . As weeks went by, I began to gain weight, and my legs and stomach seemed swollen. Deep down inside I felt something was not right, so I made an appointment and went to see my primary doctor. The doctor examined me and then did some blood work and a ultrasound and told me to come back next week for follow-up. After two weeks I went back to see the doctor, and now I was not only physically tired but mentally as well. My fingers and my face seemed to be swelling as well.

I didn't feel that things were good as I was being called into the doctor's office. When the doctor had me on the examination table, he looked at me square in the eye and said, "Mr. Zamora, I am sorry, but I have some bad news. You have a liver that is failing due to fibrosis, and you are at stage four liver disease. I am going to take you off work as of right now You *have two years to live* on the liver you have. You need a liver transplant. So he discussed with me the next phase which was seeing a hepatologist and doing more tests and then he told me something that changed my thinking I want you to go home, spend time with your wife and family." My whole world came to a stop. It felt as if the wind had got knocked out of me, and I couldn't breathe. It felt as if the walls were caving in. It rocked my world. At this point my mind was all over the place, and from this point on it was nothing but doctor appointments, examinations, and blood work. I was now at a point where obtaining things wasn't as important to me as it used to be. I began to sell things I owned. My '52 Chevy, my truck, everything I'd worked for seemed of no importance. I was concerned about my family. You know, it's funny how all the material things, all the money in life don't seem to carry as much value when you're dying. The things I'd taken for granted—family and friends—now were at the forefront of my mind.

At this point in my life, I'd been going to church for about twelve years. I mean I'd become involved in church, involved in ministry, and during these twelve years I've been extremely grateful that God has delivered me from a monster of an addiction, heroin. As far as blaming God, blaming others, even questioning God, I didn't seem to feel that way. I believe that was because I knew that this had nothing to do with God. God wasn't punishing me or paying me back for all the bad I'd done, and I've never felt He was abandoning me. Everything that was going on was because of the choices in life I'd made. Addiction is a big honking deal today and has been for a long time now.

I would say, without a doubt, my health condition came from living a life of drugs and, if anything, He not only saved me but set me free, there is a big difference from being free and being liberated. I believe there is a lot of people like this, they experience being liberated but not freedom, so in other words people are being set free but still under bondage by rules that keep them from true freedom so then people give up one addiction only to pick up another whereas never being set free, Let me be clear, we will never be perfect and sin free, and I have made bad decisions, wrong choices. So one thing I would like to say to anyone with an addiction, if you fall down, get back up, brush yourself off, and keep going forward. The addictions that we have come from something that we can't pray away. No matter how hard we pray or fast, no matter how much we serve in church or go to church, no matter how much Bible we read, we will always have our appetites. God created them, and sin distorted them. The Bible, in 2 Corinthians 10:5, urges us to take captive every thought to the obedience of Christ. In other words, we must take our thoughts, our appetites, captive, which tells me that these appetites are not going to go away. The bible uses the word "Captive" means to lock it up and bring it under submission and obey what Christ wants for our lives. I can go on but let me get back to my own story. As far as church life, I kept my faith as God kept after me.

Years have gone by, and I could no longer drive. There came a day I backed out of my driveway to go to the store, the store that I have gone to for the past fifteen years, and found myself in the middle of the street. For the life of me, I could not remember how to get to the store. It was after this that things really took a turn. My wife had a lot of people praying for me and my situation, literally all around the world from family out of state to K-Love radio station, a Christian music station where the pastors would pray daily for people. Let me just say to anyone out there who has been sick, keep in mind God always has the last word, even though sometimes we may not like or agree with what God's last word is.

Eight years had gone by, and things were getting tough. I was terminally sick, and I found myself going to church with legs swollen, feet looking like balloons, and having to put my feet up on a chair. I could have stayed home, and I know the Lord would not have disapproved, because it's not the building that saves you, it's who's in the building that matters. It's about relationships. The Bible says, "For we wrestle not against flesh and blood, but principalities, against powers, against the rulers of darkness of this world, against spiritual wickedness in high places" (Eph. 6:12, KJV). Do you ever feel as if there's a lot of things against you, one thing after another? This scripture says it all, and believe me, the battle was on, and I definitely wasn't throwing in the towel.

Regardless of my doctor's diagnosis, God had other plans, and I've outlived the original diagnose of only two years to live. It was eight years later, 2009, but I was not dead, though I was pretty sick at this point. I was no longer permitted to drive. I couldn't even carry on a conversation with people. I had a serious case of encephalopathy due to liver disease. This happens when the toxins from our liver backflow into the brain, and it can result in serious brain problems that end in death. Every time I would talk to someone, if someone interrupted our conversation, this would cause me to forget what I was talking about, forget what I was saying, which caused me to feel, if I may say, pretty dumb.

By 2010 I was no longer able to talk to people. The only one I would talk to was God, and from this point on I was in and out of intensive care for treatment of sepsis. I remember going into the hospital, and they'd immediately put IVs in my neck. Due to being septic, which is a blood infection, the doctors would have my wife sign papers and tell her I might not make it and that if the antibiotics didn't kick in, the infection would win. I thank God for His grace and mercy. I will say this, the devil might have us to believe or think he has written out the end of our story, but I know of a God who is into rewriting people's stories and showing us that He can do the impossible.

"Hello, somebody."

CHAPTER THREE

The Connection Is Dim

(If I die, I win; If I live, I win)

I t's now 2011, and ten years have gone by. I am still alive and on the transplant list. The doctors said two years, and it's been ten long years, but the connection of life is growing dim. The light is not getting any brighter at the end of the tunnel and after all the things I have experienced, I am tired. For years there was a phrase I would say, especially when things looked dim; trust me there were times I prayed and felt like, *God, where* are *you*? You see, I believe God is obligated to fulfill His promises, but He is not responsible for fulfilling ours. Believe me, every day was a battle. One minute I am up; the next minute I am down. To be honest, the past few years for me were off the chain, and the phrase I would say to myself and everyone around me was, "If I die, I win, and if I live, I win." I found comfort in this scripture, "Knowing that when we are in the body we are absent from the Lord and to be absent from our body is to be present with the Lord" (2 Cor. 5:8).

After being in and out of intensive care with blood infections, fevers reaching 108°, blood pressure dropping to a point

15

where doctors were unsure if I was going to pull through and my life would end, I remember the one thing I dreaded most in the ER was when they'd have me lie with my head over the edge of the bed so they could insert the IV into my neck. They would say they wanted to go into the main artery in the neck so the antibiotics would work faster; it was a direct line. My only comfort while this was going on was my phrase: "If I die, I win, and if I live, I win." This phrase became so much truth to me, I knew without a shadow of a doubt that the minute I died and then opened my eyes again I would be standing in the presence of God; now this is truth. It is very important that we don't trade the truth for a lie. We need to be careful when the lie comes in that we dig out the lie and replace it with the truth, with God's Word. Be very careful because when we believe a lie, we give power to the liar.

Too many people in life, even in our church's today, think just being good is good enough. They think that just being a good person, a person who helps people, gives money —now, don't get it twisted, that's key and is important—but the important message is that we accept Jesus Christ into our hearts as Lord and Savior. You see, too many people, if they're not careful, can be deceived in thinking they don't have to accept Christ, they don't have to allow God to change their lives. Sometimes it's because they feel there's nothing to change. If the truth be told, they have no relationship with God.

The enemy doesn't mind if we believe there is a heaven as long as we believe there is no hell. This is one of the biggest tricks of the devil: to get people to think he doesn't exist. The devil wants us to think or say God is a loving God and He doesn't send anyone to hell. Well, they may be right to a point. We literally must step over God to get to hell. Let me say it this way, why would God force someone to spend eternity with Him in Heaven if they don't want to spend time with Him here on earth? So we need to be very careful on the choices we make in life, God will honor our choice and If we choose not to go to Heaven, then God will honor that choice and be sure we don't.

We make the choice of where we're headed, not just in this life but in the life to come. Yeah, I know it's a little harsh. I get it, but I know without a shadow of doubt Jesus is the answer. I accepted Christ as Lord and Savior thirty-plus years ago, and my faith in God has carried me through. Keep in mind, we have our moments of doubts, fears, and anxieties.

At end of 2010 I was tired of being in the hospital for the last four or five years, being poked, my body in so much pain that I began to think, *Lord, take me home.* After this it seemed as if my condition began to worsen and fast. I was back in the hospital again, and now, deep down inside, I didn't want to live anymore. I never told my wife at the time, but I wanted to give up the fight. I was tired. One day while in the hospital I got a visitor in the late afternoon. She was the mother of Carlos, a good friend of my son from high school. They grew up together, and Carlos was always at our house. That day Carlos had brought his mom to visit. She was a woman of intercessory prayer, a prayer warrior, which means she was someone who would stand in the gap and pray for people who couldn't or didn't pray for themselves. As our visit was about to end, she said, "Can I pray for you?" I said of course. So, she prayed, and wow, she stopped in the middle of her prayer, stopped and paused, and looked me straight eye to eye, this lady whom I don't even know except through her son, and she said, "The Lord told me to tell you, 'Don't quit, don't stop fighting,'" and at that very second it felt like the room lit up. The dark cloud I'd felt was gone, and God's presence filled that room. I broke down, and I wept like a baby, and immediately after this I regained a new focus, a new perspective of how powerful God is. I began to recover quickly, left the hospital, and continued to go forward, no matter what came at me physically or spiritually.

Up to this point, the key was to continue to trust in God and, no matter how dim the light seemed to get at the end of the tunnel, to always remember:

"If I die, I win, and if I live, I win."
"Hello, somebody."

CHAPTER FOUR

Waiting to Be Connected

(The Phone Call That Changed My Life)

At around 10:00 p.m. on August 22, 2013, I was lying down in bed watching the news when my phone rang. It was the nurse at Stanford Hospital in Palo Alto, California, asking, "Is this Richard Zamora?"

"Yes, it is."

"This is Stanford Hospital. I have a few questions for you: are you sick right now? No. Have you been sick recently?"

"No."

"Have you been in the hospital lately?"

"No."

"Have you had any fevers lately?"

"No."

Then, in between these questions, my heart began racing, and my thought was something I feared, which is what the doctors looked out for, and that's liver cancer. You see, once this happens, it's a done deal; now, that's my thoughts, not God's. I asked the nurse what's this all about. Then she said something I'd waited and suffered for twelve years to hear,

"We have a liver for you; would you be willing to accept it?" My whole world came to a stop, and I said yes. She then told me I had so many hours to get to the hospital.

It was a three-hour drive from my house to Stanford Hospital. As soon as I got off the phone, I literally couldn't think, let alone figure out what I had to do. My wife started calling family—my mom and my kids—and I began to change, trying to figure out what to bring, when suddenly it dawned on me that this time I might not come home. I thought, *Here we go, not knowing if this is my last car ride.*

To this day I don't remember one bit of the car ride to Stanford. I don't remember if I was asleep or awake. As we got inside of the hospital, I felt like life came to a stop. I remember thinking, *This is it; I may leave the hospital not the way I expect.* This is when we need to understand salvation doesn't kick in when the coroner picks us up, but salvation kicks in the here and now. So, the question is when we die, what is our legacy going to be, what do we want people to say about us when we're gone: "He had a good haircut," "He was a hard worker," or "Yeah, he was good man"? I don't know about you, but I believe the number one thing people should say is, "He loved the Lord; he was such a servant, always trying to pour into people's lives."

Back to the hospital . . .

Shortly after I got there, my dad, my kids, and my grand-kids arrived. It was now after midnight, the early morning of August 23, 2013, and they began to prepare me, and then took me into a room with my wife by my side. Once again, I hardly remember to this day what the conversation was, but one thing I knew for sure, I was near death. I remembered that day in 2001 being told I had two years to live, and now it was twelve years later. Up to this point I was tired. There was no doubt in my mind that Jesus was the only reason I was at the hospital in that waiting room ready to have a liver transplant. Did certain people along the way help me, push me, encourage me? No doubt. God used people in my life to stand with me while I fought the good fight of faith; you see, in this journey walking with God we will need three types of people, people that will fight alongside us, people that will fight for us, and believe it or not, people that will push us back into the fight. I believe this is why this book you're reading is about relationships, about being in community, staying connected to Godly people.

Maybe I can't remember the conversation as I waited with my wife in that room because my anxiety was so high. This is when fear steps in, fear of the unknown; on a side note, if anyone tells you they have no fear, they're lying; only dead people are fearless, so keep in mind faith and fear always ride in the same car—the key is to make sure faith is driving and fear stays in the backseat. Around 11:00 a.m. they came in and wheeled me out. On our way to surgery, they stopped my bed by the doors of the surgery room. My wife, my dad, and my two sons were there. My third son lived out of town but came down after, to see me. You know what's funny? I can remember this moment to this day, it was so clear, I felt like the whole world stopped spinning. I kissed everyone and said goodbye, whichever door I was going to wake up on, the recovery doors or Heaven's doors.

We went in, and there were a lot of people in the surgery transplant room: doctors, nurses. I remember the doctor, Dr. Bonham, who was performing the liver transplant, and then there was the anesthesiologist. He had a bandana covering his head, he seemed like a cool dude, which he was. I remember he looked at me and said, "Relax. You're in good hands. I am going to take good care of you. Before you know it, you are going to wake up, and it will be all over, the surgery will be over," and looking back to that moment, he was right.

I will never forget the phone call that changed my life forever.

CHAPTER FIVE

The Disconnect to Reconnect

(Sometimes We Have to Let Go)

The liver transplant was done; they disconnected my failing liver and reconnected another, healthy liver. Keep in mind, if this hadn't happened, if the transplant hadn't taken place, I am 100 percent sure I would not be alive. When I was on the transplant table where this miracle was taking place, I began to think about how important it is to let go of things that are not healthy for us and above all letting go of unhealthy relationships, but true long-term healing means not just cutting people out but replacing them with healthy people. I'm talking about the spiritual transplant table of life. So many people in life have a hard time when it comes to cutting out dysfunction in their lives, for many it has become normal be very careful, because the minute we try to do this we can sabotage this attempt and keep out the ones that are truly good for us. Why? Because dysfunction always has excuses. Let's look at a good example.

There is a story about the man at the pool of Bethesda where a great number of people used to lie—the blind, the paralyzed. There was a man who had been disabled for thirty-eight years, and Jesus walked up to him and asked him if he wanted to get well. The first thing he said was an excuse. He said, "'Sir . . . I have no one to help me into the pool when its stirred" (John 5:1–7, NIV). You see, the stirring would happen the first one in the pool was healed, but Jesus didn't ask him if he had help. He asked him, "Do you want to get well?" Because dysfunctional situations always have a reason why they're unable to change it seems as if dysfunction has a repetitiveness: you know like that problem we have, that toxic relationship that we have , if not careful it will come back and give us excuses why we can't disconnect, and then that connection seems to repeat itself. And dysfunction turns into repetitiveness we can fall into routine and routine surrounds itself around things we feel can't change, if we don't deal with the situation it could be damaging.

If I had said no to the phone call to receive a transplant, it would have been fatal. Talking about the right connection makes all the difference—this is a huge deal! I remember I was in recovery after I had my liver transplant, Dr. Bonham came in and said, in all the years as a liver transplant surgeon he has never seen this; he said, "When I disconnected the old liver and reconnected the new organ, I miraculously saw before my very own eyes, it was like a wave that went across the liver, and the liver turned pink which was proof that it was successful ."

After my transplant, the doctors couldn't close my stomach because the new, healthy liver was fatty and swollen. They waited for the swelling to go down, so they wheeled me back into the ICU to monitor me. I slightly remember where I was becoming conscious but couldn't talk due to the breathing tube down my throat, so I was writing notes on a notepad to communicate with family and doctors. Three days later they wheeled me back to surgery to close up my stomach, and this is where it got interesting. It was August 26, 2013, and it had been quite a journey. They draped me in the usual surgical fashion, and then opened my abdomen to be thoroughly irrigated. The liver appeared to be a healthy pink color. Dr. Bonham closed the first layer of skin and used more irrigation in the wound and closed the skin with staples. Then they removed the abdominal JP drains; the doctors said I tolerated the procedure of final closure and was then placed in ICU as critical but stable condition three days later, August 27, 2013.

I began to have slurred and repetitive speech as well as hallucinations. I remember seeing big spiders coming down the wall. Yeah, crazy, right? This went on for about forty-eight hours. On August 28, 2013, I began to have a fever of 102–103°. I was given medication to combat the fever but continued to have slurred speech, which led to an attempt to do a CT of my brain, but the doctor was unable to do the scan because I was unable to lie still enough to get the scan. That evening I became drowsier, and my breath was beginning to become rapid with evidence of respiratory distress. An anesthetist was called to perform intubation, and I was intubated and given oxygen with medication. Immediately after the ET tube was placed inside, I dropped into bradycardia, which means my heart was slowing down rapidly. This was followed by asystole, a collapse of the heart's electrical system, which meant I was in serious trouble. My heart stopped beating. Code blue was called, and chest compressions were initiated, and I was given 1 mg. of epinephrine, which is adrenaline; then for two minutes I was given chest compressions, CPR, and after two minutes I returned and, according to my medical records, I became hypertensive and agitated and was moving all four extremities.

Within a couple more days my heart stopped two more times. Once, they gave me pushes of meds without compressions, and I came back. The third time my heart stopped I came back on my own. The question we all might ask? , "What happened when your heart stopped?" I can remember two things, two experiences, that I had. When my heart stopped the first time, I remember looking up in the corner of my room. As I began to float up, I could see both sides of the walls but there was no roof, there were just clouds. And I remember seeing my hands reaching up, and as I was crying, saying, "Take me home, Lord. Take me home," I saw a scenario take place, which later came to pass after I got out of the hospital. I also heard the Lord mention two people in my life to talk to; then that was it. The second time my heart stopped, I experienced the same thing. I saw the top corner walls of my room and no roof but clouds, and my hand was reaching up toward the clouds. But this time, as I was floating up on my back I kept flashing back and forth. I could see my bed, my room, while facing up. My bed was so neatly made, and the room was lit up bright, so clean, with nothing in it, no machines, no heart monitors, no oxygen machines, but then I began to cry out, "Take me home, Lord. Take me home"; then I began to say, "What about my wife, my kids? Who will take care of them?" Then this experience ended—that was it.

I want to make it clear when we die, there is a place called Heaven, and I can say the feeling I had during this out of body experience is indescribable, so unexplainable, that I'm here to tell you to make the right choices because after we die we do go on. Well after this I was placed on the ICU Cardiology floor. I was out for a couple of weeks, intubated on oxygen, and I don't remember much. But, little by little I was coming back. Every two hours they would come in and turn me. After a few weeks I was awake but couldn't move. All my ribs were broken from CPR, I had a big cut from one end to the other on my stomach from the liver transplant, it hurt every time I moved and breathed. I lay there not moving at all and was fed through a tube through my nose. Thank God a few weeks later I was off the machine and no longer intubated. But now it was time for physical therapy. Because I didn't use any of my muscles, I'd lost all my strength. The nurses had to sit me up to feed me. Believe me, I couldn't move, but little by little, I began to sit up and move my arms and legs more and more, and then about a month later I was able to leave Stanford Hospital. And when I left, I left on a walker, thinking, *Wow, how far God has brought me!*

I feel this chapter is essential because no matter how tough life gets, even when we pray and don't see the results in our time, just stick it out. Don't quit, don't throw in the towel. In our sufferings we develop endurance, and endurance develops strength of character, and character is what strengthens our confident hope of our salvation. I want to tell you God is interested in your character. What does character mean? It means you can be trusted. Character means you've been tested and made it through the test. People don't want to know how good our life is; people want to know how we handled life when it wasn't so good. God wants us to reflect Him in our character, and the way He does it is through the fire in the furnace of our affliction.

When the refiner purifies gold in the fire, the refiner knows the gold is ready and purified when he looks at the gold and he can see his reflection. This is what God is trying to do in our lives. Through the fires of our suffering, He wants to purify us so that we reflect Christ when people look at us. What do people see when they see you? What do they see when we go through our sufferings, our tough times? Believe me, it will happen if it hasn't already. When many Christians go through serious changes in their lives today, they wonder where God is. They feel, "If God is with me, shouldn't God be doing something?"

Don't take the changes in your life as an absence of God. Believe me, He is with you, and that is why we say we serve God by faith, not by feelings.

CHAPTER SIX

(The Right Connection Means the Right Correction)

Who's your Nathan?

As we move through life, we generally don't like people who bring correction into our lives—well, most people don't. I wrote this chapter because I believe in leadership, not just physical but spiritual leadership. There is a huge difference between physical and spiritual leadership. Physical leadership pushes people to do things they don't want to do, and spiritual leadership pulls people to do things they don't believe they can do. This type of leadership, spiritual leadership, draws people to the leader and can inspire and empower them to do what they feel called to do—big difference. We will talk more about this in Chapter seven.

Most people will not admit to their mistakes or their shortcomings—or, in this case, their sins—and when they are caught, it's sometimes too late. When it comes to having the right connections and having the right people around us, I believe the most important question we should ask ourselves is whether this person has been sent by God to bring the right correction, the right counsel, into our lives. I am talking about someone who is connected to us and corrects us without any agenda or wrong motives, someone who truly cares for our future.

There's one good example in the Bible, Nathan. I believe we all need a Nathan in our lives. You can read about this story, and I recommend you pause set aside this book and read this story in 2 Samuel 12:1–10 and then verse 13; then come back to this reading. This is an interesting story about King David and Nathan, now David, who is king of Israel, has come a mighty long way. David, when he was a young man, tended sheep in the fields and was anointed years before this story we read. Do not despise the day of small beginnings. We never know what God wants to do in our lives. So, David has come all the way to the top, and we can read when David became king by God's grace and by God's favor in 2 Samuel 5:1–3. He had the highest position in all Israel, and now everybody obeys his every word, his every command. But if we look back to 2 Samuel 11:1–5, we find out David can't handle the height of authority God has given to him; he feels exempt from God's laws. This is a good example of what can happen if we're not careful, and that is to think and feel we have arrived and don't need to answer for our actions and behaviors and we feel above the law, God's law, God's authority, God's ways. Not everybody can handle authority. We see with David that the test of faithfulness to God is how we handle God's favor. The real test of loyalty is not just how we walk with God when we're at the bottom but how loyal we are to God when he has elevated us to the top. The real test is not who we are but who we're becoming.

God's favor is not to create a bigger, better version of ourselves but to allow God to be the center, no matter where we're at in life, even when we have just been diagnosed with a disease that has put an end date on life. When life takes that hard turn downward, the question is, can we still worship not just at the top but also at the bottom? Anyone can be faithful when they need something. Everybody prays when they're sick, everybody comes to church when things aren't good, when life is falling apart, can we press on? Can we forget that which is behind us, can we press toward the mark of the high calling of Christ Jesus and thank God for all He's done for us? Can we handle Godly advice after we have achieved things in life do we feel we got it all together, let's be careful we're not blindsided by our accomplishments and begin to push away the very people that God is trying to use?

During a crisis moment, David clearly showed how he had a problem handling things. He was now the king handling things his way. David began to walk around the laws of God regarding marriage. David saw a woman, Bathsheba, taking a bath on her balcony, and he forcefully claimed her to be his wife. Wait a minute—let me explain, King David, who should have been at war with his army, stayed home, and then one day he saw Bathsheba taking a bath on her balcony and began to stare too long and instead of turning away,he then called for her. This is a serious misuse of authority and power. Bathsheba didn't have the right to say no, and she came to King David's house and had sex with him—King David, a man after God's own heart. Did she sleep with the king because she wanted to, knowing she's married, or did she sleep with the king not because she wanted to but because she knew if she refused his call she could be put to death? Back then if anyone refused orders from the king, they could be imprisoned or even executed, so in all reality, King David abused her because clearly this wasn't consensual.

David sent Bathsheba home after it was all said and done. Then he got word that she was pregnant. King David knew according to the law of Moses, that Bathsheba's husband Uriah now had the right to have Bathsheba, King David, and the baby stoned to death. Keep in mind while all this was going on, Uriah was out fighting the war for his king—yes, King David. So, what did King David do? He came up with a plan (2 Samuel 11:6–13) and here is where it got ugly. King David sent Uriah back home from the battlefield and sent him home, but that didn't work. Uriah didn't sleep with his wife Bathsheba. Then King David tried again by having Uriah come to his palace. After David got him drunk, he sent Uriah home thinking for sure he would sleep with his wife, and then, done deal, David's sin would be brushed under the carpet. But nope, the next day King David found out Uriah slept at the palace entrance with the king's palace guards. King David questioned why Uriah didn't go home, and look at what Uriah told King David in 2 Samuel 11:10–11: Uriah said, "The ark and the armies of Israel and Judah are living in tents and Joab and my master's men are camping in the open fields. How can I go home to wine and dine and sleep with my wife Bathsheba? I swear that I would never do such a thing." On a side note, Joab was Uriah's commanding officer, and he said, "My master's men," master meaning King David; note what a sign of integrity—something King David should have. King David was now desperate (2 Sam. 11:14–27); the king sent Uriah with a letter sealed to give to the commander at war, a death letter. When Uriah was killed, King David found out, and he waited a while and then sent for Bathsheba after her mourning over her husband Uriah's death.

Then he had her as one of his wives, not his wife but one of his wives, so once again King David thought he got away with it, and in all reality he did. He thought no one knew what had happened, but he was wrong. God knew.

Sometimes we think we're getting away with our little secrets in our private lives, but the Bible says, "What's done in secret will be shouted from the mountain tops" (Luke 12:3, AMPC). God knows He's got to deal with this. He can't let King David think this is okay. How does God deal with it? Here it comes: the right connection means the right correction. We read in 2 Samuel 12:1, "Then the Lord sent Nathan to David." God sent Nathan to correct David. Now most people think godly correction is punishment, but actually it is to protect us; everybody needs a Nathan, but not everybody can be your Nathan. The Bible clarifies this: "Brethren, if any person is overtaken in misconduct or *sin* of any sort, you who are spiritual [who are responsive to and controlled by the Spirit] should set him right and restore and reinstate him" (Gal. 6:1 AMPC). Your Nathan has to have a track record with God. We need to know you have a prayer life, you worship God, you study the Word. I'm not saying you have to be perfect, but you got to have a relationship with God and your walk must be ongoing. You can't correct me for something you're not willing to be corrected for, so the most important thing about your Nathan is that Godly correction produces repentance. So Nathan told King David a story in 2 Samuel 12:1–10, which is called a Juridicle (Ju-rid-i-cal) parable.

A juridical parable is a story that disguises a real-life situation in order to make the guilty party pass judgment on themselves and become self-convicted. Bam! There it is. A juridical parable is meant to bring about self-conviction by putting a mirror in front of us. This is not the first time God was trying to speak to King David, it's just that King David wasn't listening. When we're planning to sin, planning to do something wrong, something immoral, God is always speaking to us, whispering in our ear through the Holy Spirit, "Don't do it," "I wouldn't go that way," "I wouldn't call them up," "Stay away from that place," "Keep away from that thing," "Don't look at that." I could go on, but it seems as though King David didn't hear right. Those who don't hear right don't speak right, don't live right, and then don't lead right; but once Nathan came into his life, we read how King David became more sensitive to God.

If you're ready, the way we know if the Nathan in our life is bringing Godly correction and has been sent by God is this: once we've received our Nathan we have become more sensitive to the spirit of God just like David did because after this we don't hear in the bible about Nathan around anymore or David sinning. He even prays after this and asks God to Create in him a clean heart and take not thy holy spirit from him, so we need to be mindful we don't always depend on people but God. Remember: the right connection means the right correction.

CHAPTER SEVEN

Connected

(Following to Lead)

It's now 2015–2016, and I have received my liver transplant; if I may say, God has brought me as well as my spouse a mighty long way, and it's been quite a journey. The Lord has had tremendous favor on my life and extended my time here with you. When we think of favor, we think it's something good—and it is—but God's favor is totally different from favor from a human standpoint because His favor is not just about us. God's favor will always include others, and if we expect God to use us to follow Him, it's going to cost us.

I am very fond of leadership, but one thing I need to understand—we need to understand—is every great leader is a great follower. Let's be honest, as leaders we like to oversee something God has gifted us to lead, but when we talk about followership it doesn't sound the same as leadership. That's where the anointing of God lies, because whether we're following or leading, we are all called to do one thing, and one thing only, *serving*. That means, in our exchanges with others, we are either a plus or a minus. In other words, when we meet someone and our time ends and we depart, did we add into their lives, did we serve them well, did we add value in their lives were we a blessing to them, or were we a minus? Instead of leaving something with them we take something from them because we have a submission problem and feel by being submissive people are taking advantage, let me say it this way: if we have a hard time submitting under someone God has placed or is placing over us, that's a huge honking problem because submission is an invitation not only to follow but to lead as well.

A good story about following to lead that activates the favor of God is the story of Joseph in the Bible. Take a few minutes to read Genesis chapters 37–47. Yeah, I know it's a little bit of reading, but it's an amazing truth how God can use someone to make a difference and be so blessed but at the same time go through so much opposition. Joseph was able to lead while following the steps that had been ordered by God. When you follow the steps God has laid out, when you follow the path set before you, don't ever think you've got it all figured out. Believe me, following, obeying the calling in our lives just like Joseph, some of us have been chosen to walk in levels of favor to help others where they are the ones created to shift things. Following God's favor for your life was not to be popular but to be powerful, to be effective. I believe there's seeds of greatness lying dormant in our lives, and those seeds will only be activated when we're faced with someone else's need because God favors need.

Let Jesus activate the seeds in our lives by being a self-feeder, a follower who studies the Bible, and when we do this, we become table turners. Activated people turn the table of life, and everyone at their table turns with it. You may think you're incapable to be a follower of Jesus, someone God wants to use to turn the tables of life, to turn an upside-down world right side up, someone God wants to use to bring His Kingdom down here on earth. The Bible says, "Thy kingdom come thy will be done on earth as it is in heaven" (Matt. 6:10). I believe too many people think it's about going to church on Sunday and then wait for Jesus to come back. The crazy thing is as the church sits back and waits for Jesus to come back, Jesus is waiting for the church to stand up, God wants His people to see the Kingdom here and now on earth. As we follow Christ, people should see Him in us without us saying a word but by our lifestyle. Once a follower of Jesus is activated, there is a timeframe to move on it. Time has a shelf life, and if we wait to follow through, we can miss the moment and go through life wondering, *"What if?"*

Death is not the greatest loss in life. The greatest loss in life is what dies inside of us while we live. It's possible you as a follower may not be the one turning the table of life, but you may be the one to give birth to that table turner. A good story is the birth of Samson in the Bible. Hannah gave birth to Samson, and clearly, we see how that changed things. You see, greatness sometimes is not in you but in who you will bring forth. God can use you as a critical hinge in opening a door for someone else who changes the world. My prayer is that something you've read will stir you up, irritate you, feeling that something is missing.

As followers of Christ, God's favor is not always granted in the way we think it is or the way we think it should be. God's favor needs to serve someone sometimes. It's not about you, but it's about who you gave birth to. God's favor has a shelf life. We will never see it until we're exposed to it. Followership requires us to be risk takers. The minute we say yes to what God is asking from us, all of our insecurities and fears come up like Gideon in the Bible. In Judges 6:11–13 the Angel of the Lord calls Gideon a mighty warrior while he's hiding threshing wheat in a wine press. Why in a wine press, which is not used for threshing wheat? Because Gideon was in fear of the enemy. Gideon tells God, "Who am I, I am the least of my family and our clan is the weakest," and then to top it off he asked God for a sign that he's the one called to do the task and not just once but twice. He asked for a sign because this didn't make sense to him.

When God calls us to follow Him, His calling for our lives makes no sense. The thing that God is calling us to do should be something we feel we can't tell anyone because this thing, this task, doesn't fit. Gideon told God, "No way am I a mighty man of valor." God's calling is always something to tackle that we're afraid of. When God calls us, we should be horrified because at times we don't feel qualified, but terrified, because there's possibly some things in our lives to overcome, our insecurities and fears, to achieve what God is calling us to do. We know people and maybe even can say to ourselves that there is no way we could be doing what we're doing or getting ready to step out to do what seems to be impossible, and clearly, we're right. The Bible says what's impossible for man is possible for God; in other words, it has to be God. If we're going to be a great follower, a great leader in the eyes of God, stay connected to the One who is calling you. Remember, we're not qualified but were chosen and connected to the difference maker to make a difference.

Chapter Eight

The Connection Doesn't End
When We End

"The enemy is not just after you."

When I say the enemy is not just after you, I mean he's after those after you: your family, your friends. There's a lot of things we can control in life, and there's things we can't control. There are things in life that are going to happen no matter how much we try. I have six grandkids and two great-grandkids, and if you have kids and grandkids, you want the best for them. Some parents have goals and plans for their children, but for the most part we want our children to go into the right direction. We want our children to make the right choices and maybe possibly not repeat some of our choices as parents, especially the wrong choices.

All three of my sons were taught to love God, to love those around them, and to treat people the way they want to be treated, but we need to understand that the world we live in has become pretty evil, and it seems to be getting worse. There are forces at work, and if they can't get to you, if they can't destroy your life, they will go after your kids. I strongly believe the enemy is after our kids to try to bring us down.

No matter how bad things get, we need to stay fighting the good fight of faith. The one thing that can knock our faith out of balance is what I would call the theodicy moment. Theodicy is defined as the defense of God's goodness and omnipotence in view of so much wickedness, suffering, destruction, and distress. I believe the enemy, the evil in this world, is after our young people. He's hard at work to destroy, ruin, and if not take their lives by some tragic event. Let me say this, that the enemy, the one who robs us and is trying to strip off our faith, doesn't go after people who are of no value. A thief doesn't go after a homeless person to rob them. If our kids are experiencing a lot of drama, a lot of opposition, it's because the enemy sees their value.

Many think the gun violence we're experiencing—how young people are gunning down young people—and when someone dies or is put in prison, we might think, *Good, that's where they belong,* and rightly so if someone breaks the law. But keep in mind those ones also are valuable in God's eyes. God doesn't see us as we are but sees us as who we can be. It breaks my heart to see the killing of people, the ones who feel there's no hope, the ones who are in prison. Those that are greatly gifted and greatly talented are always greatly conflicted. I hope we can understand the enemy is not just after us but after those around us to get to us.

In January of 2013, I experienced something I pray no parent has to go through. It was late Sunday evening; well, let me back up. My son Michael graduated from Kennedy High School in Sacramento, California, where he'd taken administration of justice for four years. Michael was instrumental in having his Junior High School's name changed from Goethe Junior High School to Rosa Parks Junior High School. He had the opportunity to go with the teachers and the principal to a meeting with the city officials in June of 2007 and shared why this the name change of the school was so important. After he graduated high school, he worked for a year at Safeway, which is when it happened. It was January 2013, and it was a Sunday night. He went out with some friends, and the next day he was going to start college to become a detective specializing in crimes against children. I can still remember that horrible night when two of Michael's friends who had gone with Michael that night brought us the news that Michael had been hit by a car and was at UC Davis. Keep in mind, I was now twelve years on the liver transplant list and terminally sick. My wife called the hospital and was told we should get to the hospital as soon as we can. They wouldn't say more.

When we arrived at the hospital this doctor said Michael was hit by a drunk driver while crossing the street, and all I could say when I saw my son was, "My God, why?" As I walked in to take a closer look at my son, there was blood everywhere. His clothes had been cut off. I lost it. I had to walk out of the room to contain myself. Once again, my whole world came to a stop. The doctors said that Michael had head trauma, possible brain injury, broken leg that snapped in half in two places, a hematoma to his back, his whole right side was hit, and they were unsure of him surviving. I thought, *Wow. My son is in the ICU Trauma Center, and I am on my way out.* The doctors recently had told me if I didn't receive a liver transplant or a live donor within the next six months, I was not going to survive. My wife was very instrumental in getting the word out to pray for Michael. She contacted K-Love radio, The Fish radio station, who have pastors who pray every morning. She also contacted churches and friends who in turn contacted new friends, and all of them were praying. My sister-in-law in Colorado was praying, and literally people around the world were praying for my son. I can't express how important but how powerful this weapon is as days went by. We were at the hospital morning till night, and we would pray, and everyone in the trauma unit knew who we believed in and knew we were praying. I remember when we would get to the hospital, the nurse would tell us to pray; his cranial numbers were high and that indicated his brain was swelling from the impact on the head, which meant if the numbers got too high, they would have to cut a piece of his skull to allow the brain to swell without the skull causing pressure to the brain. They would freeze his skull to then reattach it later.

When we would get there to his room each day the nurse would say, "Pray again, his numbers are high," and we would be in the room walking around and praying silently, and we would see the numbers literally drop back down before our very eyes, which kept the doctors from having to remove a piece of his skull. Then he got pneumonia, and the list went on. It was one step forward and then two steps backward for two weeks. He was living hour to hour. The doctors were saying if he does live through this, we would have to care for him and would have to correct him in public it was the front lobe of his brain, that helps our decision-making, that was damaged. So, what the doctors were saying is my son would have the mentality of a toddler.

A coworker who came to see Michael a few days after the accident told us that the day Michael left work, Michael had said, "My dad is real sick and needs a liver transplant; I am going to be the one to give him half of mine." He must have known that people who need a liver transplant can get it from a live donor in a procedure where they cut the liver in half and transplant it. The half liver in both people will grow back to a full liver within weeks. When I heard Michael said he was going to be the one to donate the liver to me, it brought me to my knees.

Let me explain. One day I went to the house. I had to get some items from Michael's room while my wife stood at the hospital with Michael. I remember to this day when I got to his bedroom door and grabbed the door handle. I couldn't open it. I couldn't open his door for the life of me. I couldn't go in there. I began to cry, and then that crying turned to weeping. I lost it. I remember in the hallway I backed up against the wall, and I slowly slid down onto the floor, weeping, begging God, saying, "No, not this way, Lord. Please don't let my son die. I don't want my liver transplant this way." All I could hear were the words that my son told his coworker, "I'm going to be the one to give my dad his liver." That was a hard moment for me.

A month later my son was alive, but his memory was bad. He did not know who we were! No longer were we mom and dad but someone there who was visiting him. He had physical therapy to speed things up, and after a few years my son is now able to work and live on his own. He has worked hard at recovering from his traumatic brain injury. Am I saying he was able to obtain the career he wanted? Well, no, maybe not, but he is alive, and I am very proud of all the work he is putting in. What I am saying behind this ordeal is that the enemy is not just after you, he's after those around you, those closest to you, to get to you, to get us to lose our faith in God.

At one time or another, if we have lived long enough and served God long enough, we will possibly have a theodicy moment. A moment like this, where evil or tragedy knocks on our door, which will knock our faith in God out of balance. I mean, what do you say? It was God's will that my son was hit by a drunk driver, do I tell my son all things work together for the good for those that love Christ and are called according to His purpose? Well, that sounds good, and I believe God's Word to be true, but truth be told, during these moments those words do not help me. The reason my son was hit by a drunk driver is plain and simple. It was because someone made a choice to drink and drive. All the evil, all the tragedy in the world today simply happens. Let us not try to spiritualize things. Let us not sanitize the Scriptures and understand that all the things that are taking place in our world today are caused by the choices people make.

I believe the enemy, Satan, himself along with the demonic forces are being strengthened and enhanced by all the things that people do that are wrong and evil—killings and shootings, drug trafficking, sex trafficking, the list goes on. In the beginning, the serpent didn't come out until Adam and Eve had sinned, until they'd made a choice that went against God's will. I know what you're saying, God is in control and rightly so, but if that's the case, then why would God put a tree in the middle of the garden and tell Adam and Eve not to eat of the tree and don't look at it? If God knew they were going to do what He asked them not to do, it sounds like a setup. But it is not that. God created us with free will—we have the power of choice— and as long as people continue making evil choices, evil will continue to grow out of control. It's true. Look at our world today, how out of control it is. In the beginning when Adam and Eve sinned, it was a snake, and at the end of the Bible, Revelation says it is a dragon. Evidently, someone or something has been feeding this thing and that possibly could be why this evil has grown so much that it's out of control. Remember, when evil and tragedy comes down our street, let us choose to make the right choice. When our kids are under attack, when things in life are out of control, let us pray, let's study God's Word. Let God direct our choices. Will this make the world better? Maybe not so much, but it will make our world better and better for those close to us. When people see us living a lifestyle that chooses not to sin out of control, chooses not to do evil, chooses not to bring tragedy upon others because remember the enemy is a strategist he has been around a long time, he has studied us and he knows what we like and don't like. The enemy wants us to be busy, busy with the things in life so busy that we become numb to things around us and before you know it he has a grip on us a foothold. If were not careful this could be the legacy were leaving behind to those closest to us, remember the enemy is not just after you he is after those after us and if he can't get to us he will get to those closest to us to try and bring it all down.

CHAPTER NINE

Are We Losing Connection?

(Lights out Due to Pressing Times)

Romans 1:1–7 says that his unique identity as Son of God was shown by the spirit when Jesus was raised from the dead, setting Him apart as the Messiah. His unique identity is what set Him apart, His lifestyle, His Godly character, His walk along with His word. We can have a good talk, but it's a huge honking problem if our walk sends a different message. I believe the enemy doesn't mind us going to church as long as we keep our lights off. You know it's hard to find something in the dark, it's hard to find your destination in the dark, but when our light is on, we can clearly see where we're trying to go. It's the light that lights our path, but more important, when our light shines bright it leaves room for others to see and begin to walk in the same light, and that's the light of Jesus.

You may ask, how can I have this light? There's are two key-ways: spending time in God's Word and spending time in prayer, reading the Bible and praying. The power and effectiveness of Jesus will stem from our private life with Him, our private life will bleed out into the public life. How are we in public? how are we when opposition comes? God is not concerned with what people say or do to you, but He's concerned about how we react to them. Spiritual maturity is not an automatic process. Just because we go to church, just because we have the talk down, just because we go to a small group doesn't mean we are growing spiritually. In other words, conducting ourselves with spiritual maturity is more than having a mental picture of spiritual maturity, a mental picture of how to grow. We must be intentional to grow and be consistent with God's truth so we can treat people the way God wants us to and let him teach us how to deal with everyday life. We must be careful that we handle things in a mature way, not in a childish way. The Bible says to have a childlike faith but never encourages a childlike attitude. A childlike attitude is a spiritually immature person who meets adult situations and tests with childish and immature reactions.

I believe there's certain tests in life that mature our faith. COVID-19 was one of those tests I believe God was using. I can't say God sent COVID, but I will say He used it to wake us up. Or possibly, God was using this to change our path, change the direction we were headed, so the question is, are we still listening now that things are back to somewhat normal? Have we put God back on the shelf? Does God have to allow more trouble to remind us that we are back in trouble because we have possibly once again made friends with the trouble we're in? Have we missed the light and allowed the dark to come in? Have we traded the truth for a lie? Have we become dull in our hearing, gotten comfortable in our surroundings of everyday life, and allowed that to stunt our growth? I guess what I'm saying is spiritual maturity doesn't come naturally but must be learned. It's a learned behavior.

I believe there are some things that can cause a loss of light and develop a serious flaw in our character development, and one of those things is a spirit of comparison. Spiritually immature people fall into this if not careful. The enemy has used this from the beginning. In Genesis 3:4, the serpent had Eve compare herself to God. He pointed to the tree of knowledge good and evil, and the serpent said to the woman, "God knows that your eyes will be open, and as soon as you eat it you will be like God knowing good and evil." Boom. There it is, "you will be like God." Take note, the enemy will always tell us we should be like so-and-so, and by this he will point to something we don't have now. Why did he use the spirit of comparison on Eve? Why does he try it on us? It's because he wants to create chaos in our lives by making us feel something's missing.

The Garden of Eden in Genesis was a world of order. After Eve bit the apple, the chaos began. Anything out of order creates chaos. When there's no order, there's chaos, and chaos is something that has no form, has no direction, and it's full of confusion. God saw it from the beginning. Genesis 1:1–2 says the earth was without order and was void without form, and that's why in verse 16 God said He will make two lights, a greater one in the day and a lesser light in the evening. Both lights were just as important and for people it's the same. We are all equal in God's eyes. No one is greater or lesser, but we all have a job here on earth. Anytime the enemy can cause a spirit of comparison, anytime the enemy can cause someone to feel lesser in character, lesser in life, they will always compare themselves with the greater ones. It doesn't matter what position we have. It doesn't matter how much money we have or how much we make. It doesn't matter how big our house is because we are all equally important to God. We need to be careful that we don't allow all the outward stuff to make us feel that God is with us. Let our stuff not be registered as a sign God has approved us. Having stuff is not a big deal; what is a big deal is when stuff has us. In other words, the blessing is not in what we have; the blessing is in knowing we are all His children and that has nothing to do with what we have.

Before we met Jesus, our lives were chaos. Our light was out, and we were walking in darkness. Our lives had no form, no direction, and were in total confusion. Our lives made no sense until God stepped into our lives and created order. By stepping into our dark world, He turned on the light. God stepped into our mess so He can turn our mess into a miracle.

As I just mentioned, in Genesis we read how God created the two lights, one for the day, which is the sun, and one for the night, which is the moon. There are some characteristics of these two lights we can learn from. The moon at night will reflect the light on earth until the sun comes back. One of our responsibilities as a believer, as a Christian leader, is that when Jesus, the Son of God, is absent, until He comes back, we need to shine the light where there's darkness. That means if we're the light, then when we show up, darkness must flee. As a believer we can't stay in the darkness unless we start liking the darkness and acting like the darkness. That's why when we show up in the room darkness should flee. People should feel uncomfortable. People should stop cursing and gossiping. When the light shows up, it reveals how messy things are. Just like in Genesis, in the beginning it was the light that exposed everything out of order, out of place, that needed to be fixed. When we show up, we should show up with such light, such anointing, and such presence that it reveals any dysfunction in the room.

Keep in mind, the greater light and the lesser light worked as a team, and that's one thing the enemy doesn't want. He wants to divide us, and his line of division is "Which side are you on?" The scary thing with the enemy's line it's not a clear one, and that's what happened with the disciples. Judas was a good example of how that line wasn't very clear for him but what happened to him, how his light was dimmed, can happen to us. Little by little, the enemy was taking away everything Jesus had for him. Judas wasn't being persecuted. He was being petted, using this to cut a line between them, and that's what the enemy wants to do, cut our fuel line. He wants us to become spiritually careless, waste time, sin more, so he can harden our hearts by emptying us out, emptying out the light. The enemy rules in any areas where there's no light but darkness, and darkness means an absence of light, and an absence of light means an absence of truth.

When people are tormented, frustrated, and defeated, it always boils down to an absence of light. What is an absence of light? It's a lie they've accepted in place of the truth. This is huge because the enemy loves and thrives in darkness, and his goal is to develop strongholds. And this is where 1 Peter 1:13–14 comes in. It talks about self-control, and I'm so glad that I gave up what I had in mind to follow Jesus. If it wasn't for Him I wouldn't be here today, so 1 Peter talks about how to prepare our minds and exercise self-control so we don't slip back into our old ways and the light doesn't dim and possibly go out.

The Bible also says to be holy, in other words, to be separated, to be different, but I wonder if we are. I wonder if we asked the people around us how we are, would their responses match up with who we say we are? I believe when God talks

51

about holiness, He's talking about having a holiness of mind and a holiness of heart because if we have these two things in our lives, then we will have a holiness of conduct. But if there's one thing that we need to do in order to keep the light on, to keep the fire lit, it is that we have to make sure we continue battling, in other words, we will face conflict, and it's our conflict that God will use to push us forward. A good example is David and Goliath. If David had never had a Goliath, we would never have heard or known about David. Goliath pushed David into his purpose. Conflict and opposition will do two things. They will make us weaker, or they will make us wiser. Judas didn't understand this. Judas failed and allowed his light to go out. Judas kept blowing it, but Judas didn't betray Jesus suddenly. It was little by little. Let me say it this way, Judas was good in church. It's easy to speak faith in church, but the problem is when our faith doesn't make it to our private life, when our faith doesn't enter our character—how we treat our spouse, how we love people, how we forgive people. Judas never denied the light. What he didn't do was guard his mind. He toyed with sin, and he never exercised self-control. There was never a clear line.

I believe in life we should have a to-do list. The question is, do we have a *to-don't* list? Do we know where to draw the line? Because Judas didn't have this, he was only able to experience liberation—not freedom. Liberation is an event, and freedom is an experience. This happens often in church today because it's real hard for some people. We still love the things of the world. We still want both, both kingdoms, but sometimes our kingdom must go so His kingdom can come. In other words, Judas was going to church on Sunday and then acting like the devil all week; flipping back and forth, never being set free but just experiencing liberation, just another event. Living like this is dangerous.

In Proverbs 14:12 it says, "There's a way that seems right to a man but in the end it leads to death." I believe there are possibly some people that have been set free but don't feel real freedom. There is a story back in ancient Rome about a debt slave, the myth of Addictus. Addictus was a debt slave that was enslaved by a creditor, enslaved because he couldn't pay his debt; that's how it was back then, and once the bill was paid, they were set free. Well, this is where this myth comes in; this man was enslaved for years finally to be set free when his debt was paid. They say that he wandered the land wrapped in chains of bondage and that he could have removed his chains at any time but that he was so used to living in painful bondage that he lived the rest of his life hand-cuffed as a slave even though he was set free, and that's like most people today live. They don't lead their lives; they accept their lives, they go to church, and they have been set free but don't experience true freedom. We can fall into the same trap if we're not careful. There are four things that can take place in our lives that can keep us from being free: (1) we refuse to change; (2) we give up some things, but not everything; (3) we see worship as a waste; and (4) we believe we're getting away with it. These four things can be a huge honking problem. Let's understand the pressing times that we're in and not allow the battles we face to turn off the light and keep us from true freedom, freedom in Christ. The Bible says in John 8:36, "He who the son sets free is free indeed." Allow the spiritual fiery furnace burn off those things that aren't good for us, like how they refine gold in the furnace as the gold heats up and melts, when all the impurities, the unnecessary particles, come up to the surface so the goldsmith can scoop off the top all the junk—that's what God wants to do: melt away those chains that easily entangle us so we can walk in fullness of light for all to see, follow and let the light reflect Christ in our life so when things in our world get dark we can keep the light on. Amen!